THE EARTH MOVES AT MIDNIGHT
AND OTHER POEMS

Murray Bodo

ST. ANTHONY MESSENGER PRESS
Cincinnati, Ohio

Cover and book design by Mark Sullivan
Cover painting by Paul Thompson

ISBN 0-86716-534-0
Copyright ©2003, Murray Bodo
All rights reserved.

Published by St. Anthony Messenger Press
www.AmericanCatholic.org
Printed in the U.S.A.

in memory of denise levertov, 1923–1997

The Visit

We sat at table with olivetta bread,
peaches, cherries and a view of clouds you said
was Mt. Rainier.
                     We talked of the line
we couldn't see and crossed to be arrested
at Nevada's nuclear site.
                     "It was enough,"
you said sounding very Denise, "to know it was there."

We remembered saint Romero in your back yard
cloistered
                     with fuchsia, spirea, fern and impatiens.

We walked the lake's shore beside poplar trees
in whose sway you saw Tchaikovsky's dancing swans.
You laughed and scatted from Swan Lake *as we*
ascended steep steps to your front door.

Now I see your obituary in the Times,
your death covered with words I wish
were your new poem: another glimpse of the unseen
garden, the line you've crossed without us,
the elusive mountain's "measured self-disclosure."

Contents

v

jacob and the statue

vi

colorado river

ACKNOWLEDGMENTS

I would like to thank the editors of the following:

Sojourners, Poetry as Prayer: Denise Levertov (Pauline Books and Media):
   "The Visit," which appeared as "Last Visit," in a different draft
Western Humanities Review: "On the Verde River," "Garden," "Babel at
   the Hyatt," "The Earth Moves at Midnight"
Paris Review: "After the Earthquakes"
Ceide (Ireland): "The Poetic Line"
Cistercian Studies Quarterly: "On Hearing Gregorian Chant in the
   Abbey of Solesmes"
Tracks (Dublin): "Home Visit," "Oscar Romero"
M.O.O.N. Magazine: "Curandera" (in an altered form), "Modern Gothic"
Clifton Magazine: "The Fatted Calf"
Cincinnati Poetry Review: "No Light Apart"
St. Anthony Messenger: "Trees," "Our Lady of Perpetual Help," "Still
   Movement," "Teresa of Avila"

My special thanks to those who worked with me on these poems,
especially my mentors, Don Bogen, Andrew Hudgins, Herbert Lomas
and Richard Howard; and our ongoing poetry group: Pat Mora, John
Drury and Norma Jenckes, whose help in rewriting these poems
made all the difference.

I am deeply grateful to Lesly Thompson Federici for permission to
reproduce the cover painting by her father, Paul Thompson. No other
painting I've seen so captures the tone and feeling of my New Mexico
childhood.

My thanks also to those whose help and encouragement contributed
so much to the making of these poems: Brother Fred Link and my
Franciscan Brothers, especially my brothers at Pleasant Street Friary;
Susan Saint Sing, Debora Gaffaney, my relatives and my friends in
Gallup.

Priest, poet, professor, author of essays and meditations. Franciscan Murray Bodo dedicates his twentieth book, this new poetry collection, *The Earth Moves at Midnight*, to his friend, the revered poet/activist Denise Levertov, who died in 1997. Dr. Bodo also honored her in *Poetry as Prayer: Denise Levertov*, in which we see through his analyses of some of her poems their shared commitment to justice and peace and a shared delight in nature.

It was Denise who brought Murray into my life when she learned I was moving from El Paso to Cincinnati. I met Murray in a poetry workshop in 1989 and through the years have exchanged memories of our beloved Southwest desert as well as many poems, hopes and woes. Much laughter, too, since Murray is a great raconteur, which probably accounts for his popularity as a retreat leader.

At the age of fourteen, Louie Bodo, who became Friar Murray Bodo when he entered the Franciscan Order, stepped on a Greyhound bus in his hometown of Gallup, New Mexico, and headed for the seminary in Cincinnati, the city where he has spent much of his life.

Both of his parents were of Italian background and both the children of coal miners. Bodo's father, also a coal miner and activist for the United Mine Workers, eventually became active in New Mexico politics. His devout mother, a formidable influence in his life, who worked in a laundry during World War II while her husband was in the Marines and then at J. C. Penney for twenty-five years, read to Louie often when he was a child and instilled a love of books. An only child, Louie learned about the Franciscan Order in junior high school and early chose to follow the way of Saint Francis of Assisi.

We experience the imagination in the child Bodo throughout this collection. He's Gene Kelly, Hopalong Cassidy, an airman. And even now, when a young woman sits by him on a bus, the habit of reverie returns and he's "a young farmer/of the frontier, bringing her home /to rich land." The boy imagines exciting lives yet yearns—and these new poems are about many kinds of yearnings—for God to reveal himself. "As a boy, I imagined God / speaking from these brushlike trees," he writes, referring to junipers in the opening poem, "Home Visit," the poem that in the first line, in two words, sets a tone for the book, "Mother's ill." From *The Almond Tree Speaks* (1994) we know she wrote him weekly.

In "Jacob and the Statue," we read that at ten, he sets up shrines in the sandy hill by his home praying for God to appear. He tries to "stare the statue into speech." That boy is present in his other books, of course, in which we are privileged to hear this priest's intimate conversations with God: ". . . you found me, a boy becoming," "the way it was with you and me," lines from "Song for Christ Jesus" in his 1980 collection, *Sing Pilgrimage and Exile.*

Bodo savors language, the pleasure of rhyme, the play of alliteration and assonance. This book's title, his father's words, haunt us, for we all know dark spaces, the precariousness of life. A son and grandson of coal miners, this prolific writer also mines, smudged with ink. Poems of earthly farewells to parents and friends, the lyrical words of a priest and his vulnerability, reveal his lonely mourning. After years of following his vocation, he is unwilling to ignore irony, how he still struggles with the daily tension, as in "Via Dolorosa in a Time of War," between priestly schedules and the challenge of the present moment, a woman in need.

These poems, plungings into language for transformation, document internal and external movement and danger: water, fire, trains, ascendings and descendings, birds and their messages, journeys back to childhood, screams and silence, love, rhythms of grief, continuity, release. The stubborn courage Bodo attributes to farmers is his also, continuing to write while teaching high school, college and university students for thirty-five years as well as providing spiritual direction to many. A follower of Christ's and Saint Francis' grand tradition of teaching, Murray Bodo is a poetic teacher. We witness the sacramental aspect of writing, the sacredness of language, whether he's describing peonies or a woman in the inner city. Now no longer a full-time professor, this scholar, reader, lover of story and words, continues to chronicle the writer's work, how "words drop and plod," and then the turn when "the words with tentative flap / heave from the page."

Reading his writerly journey from the popular first book published in 1972, *Francis, the Journey and the Dream*, to *The Earth Moves at Midnight*, his words, "I'm becoming what I write," I think of the poet/priest, Gerard Manley Hopkins's words in "As Kingfishers Catch Fire," "*What I do is me: For that I came.*"

Father Murray Bodo describes his father trout fishing, casting his line artfully through years of practice. His son, a poet, patiently and reverently casts his.

Pat Mora

the earth moves at midnight

for my mother, polly bodo, 1913–1989

HOME VISIT

Mother's ill.
Safe in my sealed compartment,
mute with laryngitis, I'm afraid
to arrive and see what I can't say.

My heart grinds on metal wheels.
The twin peaks Native people call
"The Breasts of Mother Earth"
are heavy with snow.
Trinidad, Colorado.

Why is the train slowing down?
The angle tells me
mountains lie under the rail bed.
My throat tightens. Raton Pass.
A furious place. Rain flushes my car
through the narrow arroyo
into New Mexico.

Rain-reddened sand
bleeds onto the train's sides.
South by southwest, we're
heading for Santa Fe.

We pass the Pecos Mission.
Juniper country.
As a boy, I imagined God
speaking from these brushlike trees.

Like Israelites, we weave through the desert.
We enter the sandstorms
circling the foot of the mountains
named watermelons, *Sandias,*

that open, turn red at sunset,
spill and harden into lava
outside Grants, New Mexico.
Should I gather lava seed,
manna as for a medicine bundle?

A hawk glides, hunts, her belly
empty in the wind. A skinny calf,
a ranch house that leans like an ark,
prow buried in the sand of this primal sea.
The train snakes through dried seaweed,
its silver sides gleaming.

We surface into Gallup.
Two water birds rise
quickly from the Rio Puerco.
A mare romps with her foal.
Behind the soundproof window
I try to call out, but my voice breaks
whatever I meant to say.

The brakes lurch, the horses
scare. A single crow
sits on a telephone pole,
voices running through its claws.

"The earth moves at midnight,
shifts a bit so timbers break,
cave-ins happen."
                    Dad talks
nonstop, sitting on the couch
where you lay sleeping last
time I saw you. Your sweater
trembled with your breathing.

This morning we laid you in
the earth. Dad's recounting
how it was working the mines
in Gallup years ago.
He's deep, a mile down, it's 12
midnight, time to change shifts.

I wonder why he's telling
this story I've not heard
before, joisting dark tunnels
with details, like black veins
of coal, rank water dripping
from the walls, carbide lamps
dimming in thin oxygen.
He rushes to the part
where he boards the ore car for
fresh air and surface soil.

But I hear in his pauses
your respirator's wheeze,
tubes tunneling the silence
of air you cannot breathe.

> The essential poem begets the others. The light
> Of it is not a light apart, up-hill.
>
> —Wallace Stevens

1

Up-hill from the desert where you died,
the Amtrak Superliner crawls into a siding.

We stop. Wet snow weights a mountain oak.
Junipers and piñons droop.

My heart slips into your coma,
smooth and deep as the snow,
then rises with the train,
ascending from New Mexico
where I, descending, tried to come to birth.

Instead, they cut us apart, took me away.
I feel the sharp cut once more, and pray that now,
as when I was born, apart is not away
for you who taught me words were names:
"apart" for "just aside," "away" for "gone."

2

Someone's surprised my windowsill
with tiny Arizona cactus plants.
You'd talk to them, I'm sure,
as you always talked to the cactus
still burning at the kitchen window.

You cared for it like all diminutives,
even the lizards who twitched at your doorstep.
They followed you, green mottled ambiguities,
when you moved up the street to the new house.

Their spiny eyes would seem to wink at you
as your small potted cactus listened
till it outgrew its clay.

3

I see you last in memory
standing in light
watching your four rattling burners.
The dense kitchen smells of garlic and sage
heavy yet light like your hand
firm but delicate on the spoon
stirring, stirring,
the thick polenta hardening into a cake.

Quail sizzle, your pressure cooker's spout
quivers, your wrist cricks with age.
The pockets of your flowered apron jacket
sag with spoons and forks that lift and turn
zucchini and doves, polenta and venison
singing in your pans.

You spoon syllables to my lips.

I wish you could taste my words.

Is it synchronicity or something more
that here in Nashville's Crowne Plaza
I read a *New York Times* article headlined,
"Mozart Comes to Leadville"? Suddenly
you're here in this pricey room I'm now
ashamed of, knowing you never had this.
Leadville born, poor miner's daughter,
look back at me smiling, enjoying this room,
this music, this life you live in my mirror.

She stands expressionless in her smart
uniform with white apron and cap.
"Would you come back in an hour?"
She frowns and turns her cart away.

I wave it's okay now — *my mother*
waves back. A girl of twelve, she's cleaning
Nonno's boarding saloon. There aren't
other children, just coughing miners
who drink too much, stumble upstairs to
sleep, give her whiskey sips and homesick
smiles, tell her they wish they had a child
like her, to empty black spit and shine
their gold spittoons.

        When I return, she
waves from her tableau of soaps, shampoos,
gilt bric-a-brac. The room's atumble.
Puzzled, I begin to make the bed:
a rap of syllables at the door.

She's back, exiled behind another.
"Sorry, sir, want your room cleaned? This
foreign maid's confused, don't know English."

Ashamed, I nod, see my mother through
panes of glass she's washing. I'm glad she
cannot hear the words that bid her serve
someone who presumes she understands.

BIRDS IN WINTER

1

The birds are back
on the chimney next door.
Someone's moved in.
There's a fire
to warm the silo's brick
where starlings have risen
to smoke
of someone's burning.
They huddle together,
their song clogged with soot.

2

I cry in white
for some black track,
a print of paw to guide me.
Perhaps a scream
deep in the distance
to still the silence.
Then out of brush
the fox red with hunger
beside the dead elm,
its branches suddenly
a moan of crows:
I pant for home.

3

Here alone Groundhog Day
on this snow-patched road
beside the hawthorn tree,
its branches a candelabra
of robin breasts aloft
in the February sky,
I stop and study shadows
of an early thaw.
A suddenness of cloud
disturbs their stenciling.

4

I suppose every bird on wing
rose expectant, trusting in wind.
Like the hummingbird who crashed
right into our window, thinking air
was all there was before and after.

Like the crow in the sandstorm,
blown back onto the wire fence,
its head into the wind, feathers
sleek as the wings of an F-15,
claws death-locked onto the wire.

5

I cannot bear to hear
the sustained note of a bird in pain,
its cry unanswered on the winter air.

I play no Orphean lute
nor will I turn and look
to see if you're still there.

I'll pray your safe passage,
worship the God who hears your cry
as the music of your winged soul's release.

ii

modern gothic

This middle way of burning.
Perhaps it's purgatorial
or a limbo of indirection
like echoes climbing
up or down the fire escape.

Outside the bedroom window
children's voices flame.
Unattended on the asphalt,
they dance like midget Sufis
across the gridded lot
on hot macadam beds.

They break a glass at midnight
against our red brick tower
startling Compline,
my helpless, haunted prayer
enkindled between fire and ashes.

SIDE TRACK

When at last I get away to relax,
leaves wax the forest track. I slip
and fall against a stump of tree.
I sit dully, mind vacant, until

a train scares the silence,
and I'm the boy again who listens.
Freight cars couple, loud and
scary in the Santa Fe rail yards:

that dangerous desire to risk
jumping through coupled cars
stopped briefly at crossings,
death flirted with and cheated.

Screams at the back of my throat
strain for release, as when a wheel
screeches and a car's uncoupled,
shunted onto a silent side track.

I strain this time to hold on
to the sounds, find words to prevent
shunting what I'm afraid to feel
onto one more abandoned siding.

I'm back on the road, tired
of travel past towns
that try to keep bright fronts
before unprofitable fields.
Who would ever know they were
hurting, these farmers
of weary furrows? I wonder
what keeps them going, what
stubborn courage lies behind
their trim houses and barns?

The Greyhound bus bounces on
past signs that bear names
like "New Palestine." A girl
gets on at a roadside stop, sits
next to me, fixes her
headphone, rocks to Chicago.

Her arm brushes mine and I'm
now a young farmer
of the frontier, bringing her home
to rich land. She wears
a cameo brooch, calls to me
"Supper!" from the porch
of the Gothic house with its white-
wash and decent curtains.

I bump out of reverie.
The girl's hand is lifting
to music; she hums solo,
eyes wide for Chicago.

It's hard to watch the sun come up until
it's up. Gas stations and strip mall billboards
block the horizon; usual foregrounds

clutter and prevent the eye. They sprawl
haphazardly. No center, as when homes
clustered around kiva and cathedral.

Graceful trees still catch the sun, but the eye
darts to cars and trucks speeding by, intent
on work and McDonald's plastic arches.

The landscape is dizzy, mechanical.
The sick trees gather gas fumes and neglect;
their limbs tremble to truck trailers' rumble.

Then the sun clicks on; it scorches the eye,
turns to silhouette trees whose centering
rhythm our frenetic traffic prevents.

HERONS — HARTFORD, KANSAS

Standing on prairie under this tree —
a sycamore well off the road
to Hartford — I look and see
branches heavy with their load
of blue heron nests.

The Kansas sky is white,
my finger rests
on the shutter, the light
silhouettes heron baskets
in this place that shuns the human.

We're here to watch
blue heron nesting in the crotch
of trees, making the landscape
an aerie with ancient
sycamores like priests
sacramentalizing the prairie.

SALEM, 1669–1969

I reached Salem
when Eliot's cruel
April had loosened
the fan of my Ford
Galaxie's radiator.
The tick of fan
on water cooler
prevented looking for
Hawthorne's famous
Custom House.
So, leaving the metal
plaques of witches
nailed to the cold,
steel poles, I rattled
out of Salem with her
gray mists creeping in
from the sea whose salt
had choked even a bright,
smooth-running Galaxie.

He's skimming the countryside of Parma,
say, on his way to Piacenza,
and he hears again the singing rails
when they were looking together, all smiles and hails
to boys and girls waving at the train winging
past like a bullet's fast crack, their bright eyes clinging
and he holding her who made the waving hands
salutes to their good fortune. Now a damp Milan's
what he feels: the loss of possibility's
brief images as he leaves memory's cities
alone, though another sits beside him, blind
to the gun cocked in his mind.

GREAT HORNED OWL

I look up and you are there,
a silent blast of horns.
You fly away when I start
from the window.

Though it's summer,
I reach for a sweater,
pour coffee, sit,
rattle the newspaper.

Later, I feel your
heavy drop on limb.
You're back
soundless, your unseeing eyes
indifferent as searchlights.

You do see motion —
when I don't move, you move,
a loose body dance
that once again unnerves me,
though it's just you moving
to make me seem to move
so you can see me.

I turn up the radio.
Startled, you feather the air
with fearsome batons,
then sharpen your wings.

Wind constant in palm and lemon trees,
the sky a dirty grey stirring smudged
clouds over this beach abandoned
but for me walking neither into nor
away from a wind that keeps shifting.

Pelicans try to ride errant winds.
They cannot and disappear. There are
no other birds. Where do they hide, these
prehistoric-looking creatures? What
do they know of the weather coming?

Biting pricks of driven rain rattle
suddenly out of the north, the wind
steady northeast as a storm directs
the weather predictably and fear
yields to usual expectations.

Then the pelicans reappear,
fly into the driving wind.
Ancient Egyptians believed
these birds tear open their breasts
to feed the young with their blood.

Christians saw in them a symbol
of their Redeemer. I'm afraid
to ask why such sacrificial love
becomes other, more terrible extremes
in humans. O passion, O Religion!

I'm reading T. S. Eliot's essay
on Metaphysical Poets
aboard Amtrak's Pennsylvanian.
Outside Harrisburg
dark clouds cover the page:
two columns of smoke converge
in a ball, blot out the sun —

Three Mile Island.
Next stop, Lancaster.
Amish buggies, straw hats, bonnets,
wood burning stoves. My eye
returns to the page. A quote
from Dr. Johnson
on Metaphysical poetry:
"the most heterogeneous ideas
yoked by violence together."

GULF WAR GAMES, 1991

Christmas morning his son's Nintendo
was all he heard. Christmas morning and on and on.
Now, driving late from work he hears reports
of F-15's heading north from Dhahran.
It's 6:52, January 16.

He worries the car's engine home
where he ejects his son's computer hero,
Mario, for the news: further
computer simulated planes and targets.
"Why don't it work?" the boy asks, jerking
the joy-stick.
              "This isn't some game; it's real,"
the man chides.
                The boy persists. Oblivious,
he tries to command camouflaged Marios,
make them jump. Instead,
the picture explodes to electric
snow, as though
an optic nerve's been cut.

The man prays it won't
refocus into what can't be controlled
or ejected.

Via Dolorosa in a Time of War

My legs ache from walking another's
way of the cross, bearing her wooden
boxes. I speed up the pace of her move
from one dark and dirty inner-city
apartment to another,
so I can preside at the Passion
of the Lord, kiss the crucifix
on the day Jesus died.

I hesitate, turn and leave her
sitting alone amid the roaches.

I kneel before the dead Christ's clichéd
image; the woman stares back, she
and her companions, the Albanian
women who cross from Kosovo
to anonymity, their children lost,
their violators the state's evil sons who nail
no one was here where names used to dwell.

It was the silence that transfixed —
fast gliding airplanes exploding
into twin towers in fire and smoke,
the silent images violated
by commentators' voices. Muffled
carnage from where I watched cocooned
in safety, seeing with television.

Silence.
          But there beyond the screen
the cacophony the soft imploding
towers made as they seemed
to burst into a puff of smoke
like bunkers bombed on computer screens.
Silence blocking screams except inside
the mind. Silence more frightening than
sound pounding dust, glass and twisted steel.

From where we view the world's occasions
suffering is silent, and vengeance,
righteousness, righting of wrongs
is noise that cannot enter the silence
of others' suffering and death.

Silence rivets, the knowledge
of death silent, though it's making
screeches around their dying.
It is silence now that tortures,
consoles — a zone beyond noise.

GARDEN

> imaginary gardens with real toads
> —Marianne Moore

The backyard garden is not imaginary
and its toad is artificial but

something
            breaks
across
        the day lilies

an imaginary wind on an otherwise
windless day, troubling the tall, thin-
stemmed lilies and flags.

The frog begins to metamorphose,
a croaking, carbuncled and slimy intruder
real as the garden one turns away from
to make the imagined garden—all order,
symmetry, form, so to speak, except for
toads that hop out of words.

iii

anointing

for denise levertov

What to say is less a problem
than how to say it, like that old,
spreading English oak you wanted
me to write about because, you said,
it's the line I wanted so. You know,
the way it sways and stays at once.

Or the unseen tug that draws eyes
upward from the man next door
who hoes his garden in the shade
of the tree that grew without him.

Or the sound of looking down
when we work and up when we play
or say a poem or pray or look at trees.

Or the length of worry that they'll fell
the oak for spreading leaves
across boundaries where its shadow
falls on another's land
so he can't see the ordered rows
for all the fanfare rioting
in leaves that threaten his sun.

THE WRITER

Here at his desk without wings
he listens for their rush
and hears only a white hum,
fluorescent, steady, lighting
the page and the feather-like
movement of his fountain pen.

One feather is not a wing,
nor its signature angelic.
It starts and jerks in air
and the words drop and plod
aware of their labor.

Then he no longer hears the hum;
the words with tentative flap
heave from the page,
and beating grandly above him,
lift the whole lightening room.

HAEMULON

professor louis agassiz (1807–1873)

"Take this fish," he said, "and look at it; we call it
a haemulon; by and by I will ask what you have seen."
—Samuel H. Scudder

When I read Samuel Scudder's essay:
how you plunged your hand into the jar,
lifted the fish through ancient alcohol,
my own learning rose through fathoms
of cloudy liquid into the light.

I could not wait to plunge my hand
to the bottom of that jar,
soak my hand, my arm, in acrid
liquid, slide my fingers over scales,
feel what you felt, heft what you held.

So I dropped the fish back into the jar,
splashing alcohol like holy water onto the altar
where you'd left this sacrament of my compulsion
to try again: plunge and lift and look.

Look until seeing canceled smell,
neutralized it, then changed the repulsive
odor into incense, the alcohol to water,
slimy specimen to fish, looking to
tasting, smelling, listening, until
a haemulon was staring back at me,
blinking, rolling over, flashing its sides
jerking in my hand, finning outside water.

It's one more way of saving self-respect,
I guess, that when I see him at the bank,
five minutes early there like me, he's got
his check held proud between the pages
of a shiny *Truckers USA*. Is he

a trucker back in town to cash his tired
bucks? Or a wino like those he smiles for
who stand checkless in snow outside the cold
late doors of Vine Street Bank?

               We shuffle in
eight minutes after nine. He nods, teases
those who made us stand in nickel-tinted
snow until they downed their final coffee
drops. He asks one teller, "Was it hard
when bosses closed the other bank, the one
they called The Poor 'Nough Bank?"

               "Oh no," she says,
"No work to speak of there, except cashing
welfare checks." I think of all the sons who
send their mothers checks they know will bounce.
They reach out, though empty of resources,
the bogus piece of paper worth nothing
but their desire to make their mothers proud.

The teller cashes his. He seems surprised.
He turns to all the others, barred behind
their cages, wishing them and us, "Merry
Christmas." He tugs an edge of raveled sleeve,
as though he wore a brand new Harris tweed.

When I visited the monks of Solesmes
and heard them intone the plainchant
we used to sing when I was a novice,
I felt as if an old friend sat again
beside me, a welcome guest now that we
modern friars wake to the morning news.

No bells, no *"Deo Gratias"* to answer
a brother's *"Benedicite"* as he knocks
passing down the corridor. We still
meditate, but seldom together; Mass
and morning office come after coffee,
breaking an antique eucharistic fast.

Daily newspapers clutter our tables
where we talk and eat the ordinary.
We wear jeans and shirts and sweaters.
Not that chant and religious habits,
Latin and the *Magnum Silentium*,
create what monks and friars long for:

but something is discordant.
We need what chant evokes, a rhythm
learned, handed down—grace of continuity,
danger of routine—the ancient tension
of brothers before us who chanted, fasted,
found vision (or sloth) in silent meditation.

for matt and jean chimsky

It's the small domestic things
you remember after all:
morning coffee and shopping
for sensible clothes at the mall,
the shoes you buy together
and she wears home that night,
the walks in usual weather
and the silly little light
for the backyard patio tree.
Memories are quite domestic,
like his evening cup of tea,
daily decencies, not heroic
efforts to make things work.
The grand gesture fades away
and you remember some quirk
or the color of a common day.

ANOINTING

in memory of roberta tenbrink

As you summon us to your own
anointing, is it your bronze
Tibetan prayer bowl or your soul

the sandalwood striker sounds?
And when you ascend the pulpit
to speak of cancer, is it your

words we hear, or some
angel's, words that whisper and waft us
like prayer flags

to Kathmandu? And your tears —
do they really shine, or is it mine
seeing your smoldering wick catch fire

like a solitary climber the sun
suddenly strikes on the shadowed
face of Everest.

PHONE MESSAGE

in memory of john wojtowicz, o.f.m.

You died on your feast day, March 8.
Today, May 6, you talked to me.
The answering machine clicked on
and your sweet voice informed me
that I had reached the friary
and gave me several options.
One of them was your own number,
an extension I knew would not
be answered. I hesitated,
though, and wondered, would you hear me
somewhere, if I left a message
the way people do when they pray?
But fear that someone would think me
crazy sealed my lips; I hung up
the phone but dialed again, to hear
your voice, in case you decide
to answer any messages.

ADLESTROP

after edward thomas

A sign announces Adlestrop:
The haycocks' stare and birds aloft
Poised as for some punctuation
To set them free of this station.

No railway now. My car idles
At no crossing. A dog sidles
To the door, listens. The motor
Hums; what's here is not in Fodor.

It's in your poem, "Adlestrop."
Its directions define this stop.
An imagined whistle-scream
Derails the waking dream.

COUPLES II

That rose opening
atop the chiffonier
silent, still,
so unlike those
who move cerebrally
about the house
making each other
feel responsible
for their unfolding.

Fear of mere being
makes me do
while the roses
become
till they disappear.

The white orchid
did nothing
to interfere;

it is
(after the roses'
dropped petals)
still there.

I'm off doing
what doesn't see
the roses growing
or the orchid

hidden
between the roses
with its
silent eye.

for the old oak that yearns
towards the feathered clouds,
its branches not yet in bud

for old age
that still burns
with upward reaching hands

for saplings that gird
the tree's heavy limbs
and thick trunk

for a straining against roots
that encumber
something rising

for what doesn't rise
but trying, breaks open
in a flutter of flowers

HUTCHINSON ISLAND

for bob and heidi

Walking the beach with gulls, their small chests
puffed up importantly, I smile
as they stroll, hands (if wings were hands) crossed
behind their backs like Italian men
at their evening *passeggiata.*

Pelicans skim and dive for fresh fish,
the gulls scavenge for beach leftovers.
Plovers nervously flit and skitter,
water-shy whenever waves
threaten their balletic legs.
We're all here together, they working
to stay alive, I to be alive.
We are our names: beach, birds, humans.

The tide rises, waves become their name.
Is there anything more important?
Maybe the man with the two dogs, or
on this gray day the way the sun breaks
through and flashes white on the waves
where surfers ride, trying
to change their names,
or the gull who stops scavenging
and wings over the water like a bird,
or putting down my pen to stare.

A gull who's picked up my dead cigar,
spits it out with a disgusted shrug.
I cough and inhale the fresh sea breeze.
A tern butts its head into seaweed;
I sit and run my fingers through sand.
Why don't we live where the sea meets land?

iv

by the sea

TREES

to Christ Our Lord

Yours the silence
of trees
standing singly,
vulnerable
to insects and birds
and disease,
and the wind
stinging Your limbs.
Your human friends
stand together
on earth
looking up,
not knowing
how to ease
the ache of branches
upward reaching
in their ecstasy.

If you say to this mountain, 'Be lifted from your place
and hurled into the sea,' and have no doubts, but believe
that what you say is happening, it will be done for you.

—Mark 11:23

The road from Toledo to Avila:
the feel of sagebrush and cactus
where olive and pine like giant
broccoli grow.

Stone castles look like adobe
pueblos and you go up and up
through rock and mountain
barren but for poppies and broom
sweeping you higher to incongruous
beds of lavender.

This altitude dizzies but does not
purify. This climb is outside
to the high city of Avila, not
the climb inside, up the mountain
soul becomes when you try
to move it into the sea,

move it or climb it or enter
its narrow cleft that widens
through cool adobe tunnels
into a crystal cave,
an interior castle.

Young, I prayed before your icon,
saw myself your very son
safe in your arms.

Older, I see not me
but the child Jesus
whose sandal's undone.

Huddled in the crook of your arm,
He holds on, head turned toward
something, someone, chasing after.

You seem turned for help to us
who've come to you for yours.
Or do your eyes presage later sorrow,

when He and we alike fall down,
no longer children holding on,
yours the lap we're laid upon?

OSCAR ROMERO

When they sang the funeral Mass for Oscar Romero
there wasn't room for all the campesinos
in the church. Many stood outside. Like Moses
they took off their shoes for the Compañero,
the Breaker of Bread, who lay there broken, too.
The soldiers came sprinkling lead,
the shower broke the ranks of the worshipers.
When they silenced their aspergills
there were bodies, and pocks of bullets
in the walls, as usual, and—filed
like rows of witnesses—the empty shoes.

ST. FRANCIS COVERS CHRIST'S WOUND

When he was dying, he placed his
bandaged hand over the wound
in his side, and turning his bright face
to his brothers, he said, "The Lord
has shown me what was mine to do;
may Christ show you what is yours."

How relieved they were he covered
his wound, for who could follow
such suffering, or invite Christ's wounds
praying: "May I feel in my flesh
your crucifixion and in my heart
your great love that embraced it"?

Now they are free to cover their
own uninvited wounds, to love less
heroically like the *Purple Flower*
which blooms and drops its flowers
every day, that small death and rising
enough, though no one sees.

DAVID

In the nine-month strife
and prayer for the child's life,
in sackcloth and ashes apart,
the wound of guilt for Solomon
opening your anointed heart,
preparing it for Absalom,
you become our conscience
suffering sin's consequence:
pleasure to pain to wisdom.

You say
he's gone for good this time.
I say
may the whores take him
though they deserve better.
But
I know he'll come back;
you can count on that.
I'll stay here and work the farm
and you will pose at the end of rows
and wait for the prodigal's return.
You'll treat yourself to questions
about what you did wrong with the boy
and take me dutifully for granted.
Fidelity never gets your attention
the way infidelity does.
Infidelity says something
about you
that will make your guilt
run out to the fence of forgiveness
and wait for him to come back
grateful for your gift of calf.
I stay here and work
and give you about as much notice
as you give me. We both know
the fuss you'll celebrate
with robe and ring
when the boy comes home.
And when he does,
I'll give you
the look that says
I know who owns the boy now
the way you'll never own me.

Unlike New Year's silver ball that will
descend at midnight, the Easter star still
varies—moveable feast that it is.
Nothing may ignite; perhaps, a slow fizz
like one's own anticipation deflating.
The heavens' gifts bring what they bring
when they will, not when we determine.
Pentecost exploded in a galaxy of Christian
Feasts; now it moves in orbit like any star,
not moving earthward where we are.
Feasts move predictably like the Milky Way.
We watch, pray they'll explode again, splay
open the heavens, drop fiery fragments earthward,
or at least, send a sign something stirred.

PLAINCHANT PENTECOST

Sunday morning's readings spark
faith, as of fire, hot yet soft
like light insinuating
hope—dare we open our mouths,
blurt out burning syllables?

We trust instead proper notes,
ancient canonical words.

Slowly, the strict tongue's measure
opens the mind's refusal,
loosens what medievals bound
in careful notes: ecstatic
diapason—the Divine
Consonance, God's Spirit.

STILL MOVEMENT
(Motets I–V for Pentecost Sunday)

You have gone the way you came
burning in and out of the dark.

My eye searches for a horizon
to free my mind from prison.

The day, gray with backward growing,
the sun rising at sunset.

And you return the way you left,
a crack of light happening:

Out of the dry, barren heart
the shoot of something green.

By the Sea

1

Your face lighting the darkened beach
of nets and skiffs, your face
watching, what is it,
our fishing or yours?

Looking up
we feel you seeing us
stirring like water.

2

A summons in the eyes.
We drop our nets
heavy with salt
and rise from sea water
onto the sifted sand.
We hear our names:
who we are
who we will become.

3

Homeless yourself
you create a home
and we are drawn
as to a hearth
against the outer dark,
the inner chill.
The moods of the sea
a weak threat where you walk,
an ark on water,
a tent on land.

4

At first we are loath
to look at you
or listen to your words.
We're afraid of becoming your word,
of hearing our name in your voice.
We are two faces
and you are the inner one
stronger, pushing on the skull,
the skin, reshaping
the countenance we wear
the reflection we see in water.
We're afraid to talk
lest the word escape
and we lose our faces
or yours.

5

When spring comes that first year,
we watch the fig tree budding
and more than flowers
bursts forth on branches.

Lessons fall in petals
onto the palette of sand
forming a pattern
you decipher for us
and which we sadly
forget in autumn
when we need to remember.

6

We realize
almost too late
that your mission
is particular contact
with local lives:
hearing the widow of Nain
when you could be
talking to Rome,
wasting the time of redemption
with a leper in one of the towns,
refusing the general healing
in favor of some Gerasene.

7

Dying
you make sea-storm
and earthquake
pulse through our veins.
Our heads
swelling with tempest rising
beat against Jerusalem's walls
a hopeless chorus.
Your words
are arias of pitched truths
we cannot harmonize
in tempest.

The boat strains,
wave-beat without,
betrayal's cacophony
and jealousy within.

The broken notes fall
from the scale and sail
of our foolhardy climbing,
fill the hold of our hopes
with their dying vibrations.

The boat's beam
is thrust into the cracked
and broken earth.
Crossed with spar
the boat trembles
with your dying cry
that stills the storm.

Your arms suspend
embrace the world
draw life anew
from the silenced sea.
Out of broken earth
the God who fell
begins to rise.

We at sea
cling to our planks,
drift with the tide
onto the whitened shore,
the drama just beginning
as we crawl onto clean land.
We find our legs
climbing the hill
of your descending.
New harmony pounds,
foot-fall on this skin of soil.

8

You sit by the sea,
a small fire and one fish
and no clouds
aflame with angels.
You wait for us
to row toward you
your human hand,
stirring embers.

We cast our nets
and you cast demons
into the sea,
the fish indifferent victims
like those surprised,
caught between your casting in
and casting out.

9

Is the fisherman drowned,
gone down to death?
We strike the rock like Moses —
blood and water flow out,
run down the hill to the sea.
We part the waters
and walk their linen bottom
to the foreign shore
where you sit cooking fish.
And you're revealed again
when we partake of food
become your signature.
The fisherman is now the fish
and we the fishers of God.

jacob and the statue

NONNA

When I was five, I used to imagine
her doll-like cottage was inside her name.
Nonna became the house I would dream in.

Nonna was all light, even in Winter.
White wasn't color but the feeling
of name that was home, *Nonna Katerina*.

When I was six years old, they said she died.
No one believed me when I explained
that she'd only moved

into her windowed porch. I never told
how I'd go there mornings
and hold her holding me inside her name.

NONNA'S SONG

(On the Train Passing Verbaina-Pallanza, Lake Como)

Her soprano stays with me,
even now I'm sixty-five: *Entra, ballanza,*
no bella citta, se mangia, se beve,
allegre s'esta. I was four or
five, and she almost my age now when
I sang it over and over
again; and when I tried to translate it years
later, I thought it meant, "Enter, dance
into no beautiful city; eat, drink, have a good
time there." Then one day, paging a Baedeker
of Northern Italy, I saw *Pallanza;*
and Nonna's lilting word, *ballanza,* to dance,
became a city one entered; logic changed
no bella to *la bella,* the beautiful.
"Enter Pallanza, the beautiful city."
I like "dance into no beautiful city" better.

So why translate a childhood song remembered?
Is it lack of logic that children repeat
words just as they hear them? As a child
I would sing, "Tell me the tales that were told
log ano, log log ano, log log ano," the nonsense
of it making as much sense as "long ago"
because that's what I heard Mrs. Findley,
our music teacher, singing.
When do we stop hearing what we hear
until it makes sense, having been translated
in the brain to words and sentences that dull
sound to common sense? Then the mystery,
the sound logic of log ano, is lost to the ear,
and lost, too, is Nonna's voice and face
restored by words I hear her singing just to me.

Back of the old brick kilns we plotted
what now we can't remember, the three of us
scared of our own scheme—to blow up something?
Success evaded us, but not our due.
Someone called the cops and we were harried
home.
      Stubbornly, the stunt's acoustic balks.
Inconsequence bricks up the chamber where
liminal dares pushed us through the oven's
door.
      There we danced on the cold, flameless floor,
our reward a refractory passage
we can't remember after fifty years,
except to ask, "What was that brickyard thing?"

How could we have known (boys playing games)
of distant ovens, real as their flames,
that burned more than memory?

The peonies—they
were so tall,
the sun falling
through their greeneries,
or I was so small,
a boy calling
for something out of the sky
those fragrant afternoons
I thought the flowers
would take me there.

He's packed his little suitcase,
a bulging brown checkered promise.
He tilts his white sailor cap—
Gene Kelly in *On the Town*—

and side-steps out the door toward
where movie stars always stand,
by the side of the highway
lipping a cigarette, thumb

pointing toward a better life.
He waits for her car, the blonde
girl who's gonna be his wife.
A car stops, but it's only

Daddy again, who opens
the paddy wagon and speeds
him away, siren screaming.
Then—it's Hopalong Cassidy.

He puts on spurs and Stetson,
rides out of town and waits for
the white horse and black rider
he sees pounding right toward him.

Daddy's stagecoach stops instead,
and he's whisked away to bed.

GROWING PAINS

Last year their hair,
cropped at the top of their
frilled collars, they sat
in desks and chairs that
were in front of his who feared
them and said they were weird
little girls with chubby backs
that invited his furtive attacks.
He dunked their pigtails
in ink, and his dirty nails
pestered their delicate skin.

Now they're suddenly thin,
and, turning, change the stone
of mischief he'd have thrown
into a frog bloated like him with
blemishes and self-fulfilling myth.

You surprised me, writing as you did.
Fifty years! Can it be that long
since I acted skits on your porch?
And did I really steal flowers
from my mother's Easter hat for you?

You write, "I was so happy, though I
don't think your mother was."
                       I wonder,
was it just the flowers that made you
happy, those odorless props
I tossed at your shiny buckled shoes?

You don't say. You didn't then. Oh, well,
maybe it's time that gives them fragrance
and distance that gives me license to ask,
"Happy, too, because they came from me?"

They came to town Saturday afternoons,
the crazy old man and the boy.
They descended from Sky City,
the Mexican section of town. The boy

wore old-man's shoes, high topped, laced tight,
his pants hitched up to his armpits
almost. Old man, older boy, they
spoke to no one, never responded

to shouts of *locos*. Obscene gestures ushered
man and boy across railroad tracks.
Who were they? Where did they come from?
Questions I now try to answer and find

my answers betray guilt and amazement:
those we mocked as children return
years later, their shadows become our own.

JACOB AND THE STATUE

When I was ten,
I set up shrines like Jacob,
who wrestled an angel.

I'd climb the sand hill
across from home,
and find a cleft in a rock.

There I'd place my three-inch statue
of the Infant Jesus of Prague
and a tin can with desert flowers.

That way, if anyone saw me kneeling,
they'd think I was looking
at something in the rock.

On that hill, staring at Jesus
in his royal vestments of fine silk,
bordered in gold brocade,

I prayed and prayed
to make God appear.
I'd squeeze my eyes shut,

then open them fast,
to make the statue seem to move.
But the silence burned like the sun

and I'd take the lifeless Jesus home,
quiet as God.
The flowers withered in the dark cave,

until another saint
sent me up the hill again, to try
and stare the statue into speech.

When I was twelve, me and Mrs. Bertinetti would
walk the dark of Princeton to Wilson Avenue, she
to St. Francis Church and me to the convent where I
served Mass at 6:30 and with eyes in back of my head
saw Srs. Jean & Damascene, Limbania, Elise & Josephine
starched upright in prayer. The sun's first rays
fired the altar cloths, white as the Angel's wings
of the Holy Card tucked like a secret in my Missal.
Somewhere between those mornings when Mass illumined
our faces, and I wanted to build tents to hold back
glory from disappearing—it disappeared.
Christ still rises in the Host, but the Missal holds
few secrets and the shine's not there, as for the boy
dazzled, his back to nuns winged with white wimples.

for maria ramirez

Earth, red and glazed after rain,
seals your body in Gallup clay
that dries hard as pottery.
Your grave's a sunken bowl,
its lip cracked where the ground shifts
from abandoned mines below.
I kneel and draw from the ground's
mouth what mere clay cannot hold:

Your hands roll enchiladas,
soak tamale corn husks.
You raise your eyes to those
of the Sacred Heart of Jesus
ablaze in His shrine. Your palms
pat corn tortillas that bake
to shells a little boy fills.

Your small hands gather healing
herbs, work them into a paste,
smooth the poultice that soothes,
warms, then cools hard as clay.

Another rain swills your grave;
the clay begins to soften.
Flowing mud smooths, tries to seal
what the cracked earth opened.

But you keep drawing me in
through layers of soil toward
the vein of coal your husband
worked deep in the earth

you both inhabit now. I
ride the coal car down, bring
to the surface ore, poultice cool,
warming to memories of you.

IN MIDDLE AGE

come peregrin che tornar vuole

—Dante, *Paradiso*, I, 49

1

Each discovery is a remembering:
the stones of San Marco
float in the morning mist,
and he sees himself a child,
a boy after playing, who sat
and made the red and distant rocks
ships about to sail for Italy.

In Venice he is still
only the boy who dreamed of the man
standing here waving at the duomo
steaming back to America.

2

Is it too late, even though
the poppies grow all along
the side of his train
speeding toward Florence?
He's beyond the magic middle
that's supposed to slice
end from beginning.
He reaches back to catch
the longer part threatening
to un-couple.
And like the pilgrim
who wants only to return
he tries not to arrive.

3

Rome. A black cover
of cloud heavy with rain
strains out a few weak drops.
His eyes wander
windows opposite his.
A signorina opens
tightened and louvered shutters
and steals
onto her balcony.
She leans and waves into the piazza
her hand absently drawing close
a loosened robe.
Her feather duster
skims wooden slats
like those he strains against.
She disappears.
White sheets tumble
from the room where
he imagines
tight hands loosen.

4

In Assisi, surrounded by his books,
he looks out the window less
than into the pages of those others
who look up even less than he.

Always it is into the words
he leaps for that which keeps his compass steady,
south of Florence, north of Rome:
a ballast for the red rocks tilting in the sand.

How naive to think
he could cross it,
so dangerously close:
a surprise precipice or the sudden
drop from the sky, the plane
almost arriving, the boat almost
across the sea. Yet not falling,
not sinking, but imagined:
that's what widens
the divide inside, making
the crossing less and less
realistic, less and less a hope,
a dream even. And then he
no longer wants to try
because he knows it cannot
be crossed: it can only
threaten him with images
that make their own scenarios:
his plane plummeting to earth,
his ship sinking into the sea.

        He looks up and
(always) the steps are still there.
He hasn't boarded. The sun
blinds off the silver door
locked like a tabernacle.

colorado river

for my father, louis bodo, 1914–1996

LINES

1

You sit on the edge of the bank
tying flies that look like those
you see the trout are jumping for.

I sit on the edge of the chair
tying words, listening to their
artificial hum, hoping

to sound them in a line that sings
like your fly line, its signature
swishing across the river's lips.

"The more natural the action,"
you insist, "the sooner they'll bite."

2

I feel a tug on the line,
the knot of the leader slips,
the hook is swallowed, the line
broken. I try to remember the feel
of what it was that took
the barbed fly before I could
reel it in, see what it was
you wanted me to know.

PANTOMIME

I dream you
and Nonno before you,
deep in the earth mucking coal.
You surface, faces
black, as you shuffle across
the stage and disappear.

Over and again from some
dark hole you emerge, vague
behind smudged make-up,
your lamps a carbide stare.
White lips puff
under your helmets' glare.

You are a boy three years old
sailing from America
back to Italy.
Mama hugs you in the hold
where it's dark, no windows
except for her eyes.

You return to San Mauritzi
where Mama was born.
Soon her eyes turn grey:
They put her picture on the tomb,
Katerina's cameo.

Then Papa marries "Strega,"
the witch who packs you
like her portmanteau.

Your return to America
when you are six years old
is no easier, though Mama's
where she asked to be, and you're
getting used to no hand to hold.

COLORADO RIVER

After we lay you in red clay
deep in Arizona,
we travel to Grand Canyon;
stand as at your open grave,
its river-whorled strata
stretched like your stories,
their pentimento
cracking.

I see beneath strokes
tight as skin weathered, brittle,
your lips
distant as the Colorado River,
their stories silent,
removed from the dangerous edge
we lean away from, holding on
to rail and tree as we strain
to watch rafters scud
past the narrow cleft,
their mouths open in ecstasy,
their shouts unheard.

DRIVING HOME

Your station wagon strains against the wind
eastward, away from your grave's red clay
scooped out, strewn across New Mexico.
The pink bird saved from your funeral spray
dangles from the visor, the wind mill is still
in the variable air as I speed my escape
into a Kansas dust storm. No Oz or Superman
whirls round, but Navajo memories drape
me like the blankets of sand we'd fight driving
toward Kayenta or back to Gallup, sheep and cow
dangerously crossing before the careening Chevy.
I was never afraid with you at the wheel. Now
speeding, I can't race ahead of driving alone.

It's your sayings I remember most.
Like the time I drove you to Phoenix
and the doctor delivered his sentence,
"I'm afraid you'll never see straight
with that eye the way the surgeon
botched it," and you on the way home,
"See the moon, how it tilts just enough
to hang a powder horn there? That's
a wet moon, old hunters used to say,
time to stay home, and not go hunting.
And see the three stars in the moon's ring?
Means the storm will hit in three days."

When I left, I watched the wet moon ride
the plane's wing. I imagined you saying,
"See how the doctor's aim missed yet hit
the bull's eye? Guess that means you miss
what you hit under a wet moon."

Buffeted by wind,
swirled inside twisters where
Navajos say legends begin,
I used to play war
in the cockpit of an old Dodge.
Its door was stenciled
with Japanese Zeros I'd downed.

At recess I'd muster troops,
open the Japanese parachute
you sent from Saipan
and dispense handfuls of cords
to the "airmen" of Washington School.
We always let go
before ballooning silk
lifted our third grade into air
heavy with enemy flak.

After school I'd go to the Santa Fe Depot
and wait for mother to get off work.
At 5 o'clock I'd walk her home
from the laundry
where she pressed and folded sheets.
We'd talk about school
and what we were going to eat.

Some evenings I'd go back
to the train station
and double-check on troop trains,
just in case.

Once, a marine jumped off the train.
I knew you from the picture by mother's bed.

Fly-Fishing Ghazal

I see you still standing knee deep in trout-rich water.
Your hand-tied fly arcs through air, then touches trout-rich water.

I keep the image of you fishing, your waders on, your canvas hat
crunched down on your bald head, your eyes testing which water

upstream or downstream to wade through for trout waiting there
for the fly you've tied to mimic what flies above rich water,

deep or shallow, straight or circuitous. Insects around you
fly with your artificial fly, smooth and slow, then twitch, water

dimpled with their signature. The fish, confused between art
and nature, choose your flies equally, the trout-rich water

poorer for your filling creel. You taught me your art: what flies
without you leads your well-wrought fly into trout-rich water.

I thought of you again this morning
as I watched a sandhill crane walk this
Florida beach: how the year after
mother died, I sat on the Verde's
bank, watching you cast flies. A sandhill
crane teased the water, dipping her bill.

Alike on spindle legs, you and the crane
mimicked one another's slow Tai Chi
as you shadowed the elusive trout.
The water swirled and eddied
into a dream I'd dreamed the night before:

You and I beside a rough river.
A tornado bears down upon us,
whirls us onto a fretwork girder
beneath a bridge. You slip like a fish
from a creel, slide into the river.
You don't surface, and in panic I'm
arched to dive in, but freeze when a young
girl surfaces, suspended waist high
above her own reflected image,
clear in river water smoothed and calm.

I was trying to decide about
the girl, hair bobbed like mom's at twenty,
when the splash of hooked trout startled me,
its panic waking me to the fact
of your tumor, the leaden sinker

that sank the dream till now. Again I
see the surgeon cutting the sinker
from the line, you rising like the girl
for a while, flapping free as a crane.

Now the sandhill crane surprises me,
reappears here by the ocean, miles
and years away from Arizona.
And I imagine you swimming with
her, the metamorphosed girl who rose
when you drowned. Clarified images
surface from water I almost see.

GROWING HARD OF HEARING

1

How far I've come from their words,
Mother's vowels round like her rosary beads,
Dad's consonants cutting through his teeth
like the crack of his .270 Winchester.
Now here I am, academic years away,
using words the way I've read them,
my hearing now fainter than when Mother
read to me and Dad told me stories.

2

I'm becoming what I write.
And you I love—you, too,
are becoming words that hide
inside the covers of books.
Fewer sign the check-out cards,
and so these words will go
the way of the dust we're made of.
You, my mother and father, and I
your only book, all three become words
I'm the last to preserve. But why
do I need to save the words?
Maybe I'm trying to talk to the dead,
hoping you might read and remember
what's hidden inside the covers of books.

This collection of poems reflects a journey of some twenty years culminating in my sixty-fifth year, a not insignificant year for a writer—or for anyone. The poems have undergone several metamorphoses with many revisions over the years.

The present shape of the book, beginning with the death of my mother and ending with the death of my father, binds, as within the covers of a book, a self-contained experience. An experience of earthquakes, real and metaphorical, that opened and closed the ground of my being. An experience that skewed my vision for a time. An experience of the sea, both as a healing presence and as deep water I crossed several times between New York and Southampton, retracing my grandparents' crossings of the Atlantic from Italy to America. An experience peopled with Jesus and the saints, with remembered childhood friends and acquaintances.

And as I was walking and composing these words in my mind—in Eden Park (how apt the name) above the inner city where I live—a doe and a fawn came out of the woods to feed, seemingly oblivious to my passing. I stopped to watch them eat, the bright September sun like a halo around their brown fur.

Tranquil in their absorption, they looked up only occasionally at my still advance. Ears cocked only for a second as if to see if I was still there, they relaxed and returned to the grass and foliage at their feet. Then slowly, as if they'd only come to let me know, they sauntered back into the woods.

When my father died two deer, a buck and a doe, came out of the woods where I was visiting in upstate New York, and I felt somehow consoled, as if my mother and father had sent them, just as now I know something has been restored, some completion, a further peace.

And as I descended the hillside, the cry of a train from across the Ohio River triggered the childhood memory of the sounds and rhythms of trains. In Gallup, New Mexico, where I lived as a boy, the melancholy sound of train whistles arriving and leaving shaped the tone and texture of poems I was to write years after those first soundings in the ear: train whistles, the sounds and rhythms of train wheels over tracks, those clickings and clackings, regular and irregular, that led me away but bring me home again.

Murray Bodo
Eden Park, Cincinnati, Ohio

In "The Visit" on page iii, the phrase "measured self-disclosure" is from "Noblesse Oblige,"one of Denise Levertov's last poems about her beloved mountain. Cf. Denise Levertov, *This Great Unknowing: Last Poems* (New York: New Directions, 2000).

In "Babel at the Hyatt" on page 9, *Nonno* is the Italian word for "grandfather."

In "By the Sea" on pages 57–61, in explanation of the phrase, "The fisherman is now the fish," the Greek word *Ichthys* is an acronym for *Iesous Christos Theou Uios Soter,* Jesus Christ, Son of God, Savior. Thus the fish as a sign of Christ.

In "Nonna" on page 76, *Nonna* is the Italian word for "grandmother."